This book belongs to:

_____

_____

_____

_____

_____

Hoosier Heart

WRITTEN BY LUKE MESSER
ILLUSTRATED BY JENNIFER MESSER
EDITED BY NICOLE NORTHCUTT

A story about Hoosiers and the great state of Indiana

To the real Emma and Ava
and all the other children who
call Indiana home.

Thank you Indiana Historical Bureau, State of Indiana, for graciously allowing us to use its historical summary of the word "Hoosier."

Thank you Christina Pippen at C.J. Pippen Design for your creative talents, continuous candor and professional work product.

Eva Publishing LLC
345 W. Broadway
Shelbyville, Indiana 46176
www.evapublishing.com

Book design by Christina Pippen
The text of this book is set in Big Caslon.
The illustrations of this book are rendered in watercolor on paper.

Printed in Indiana, United States of America

First Edition

Library of Congress Control Number: 2006906073

ISBN-13: 978-0-9786799-1-0
ISBN-10: 0-9786799-1-1

Order autographed copies of *Hoosier Heart* and other books by Eva Publishing LLC by calling (317) 697-6615 or visiting our website at www.evapublishing.com.

This is Emma and Ava
and their friend Ben.

Like most children, Emma, Ava and Ben
like to ask tough questions.

Her father took a long pause and said:
Hoosiers are a lot of things.
They come from our home state.

We're known for liking basketball.

And, our auto racing is great!

Hoosiers live across our land from South Bend to Evansville, Terre Haute to Richmond, Gary, Greensburg, Bloomington, Muncie, Lafayette, Fort Wayne and Jeffersonville.

• Gary

• South Bend

INDIANA STEEL MILLS

NOTRE DAME

• Fort Wayne

TIPPECANOE BATTLEFIELD MUSEUM

VICE PRESIDENTIAL MUSEUM

• Lafayette

• Muncie

INDIANAPOLIS

Richmond •

INDIANA BASKETBALL HALL OF FAME

• Terre Haute

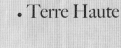
GEORGE ROGERS CLARK MEMORIAL

• Bloomington

• Greensburg

• Vincennes

WORLD FAMOUS TOWER TREE

LINCOLN BOYHOOD HOME

CORYDON STATE CAPITOL

NEW HARMONY HISTORICAL SITE

• Jeffersonville

• Evansville

Some Hoosiers work on farms,
where they grow corn and soybeans.

Other Hoosiers make new things
in all our factories.

Hoosiers enjoy
Christmas
all year in
Santa Claus...

...and have
a circus
in Peru.

We swim
on the
beaches
of Lake
Michigan...

...and ski
in Paoli,
too.

Hoosiers are known for great music...
just ask John Mellencamp.

And, Hoosiers play other sports, too.
The Colts are our football champs.

Indiana University is a school for Hoosiers, but Hoosiers learn at other places, too...

small schools like Wabash, DePauw, Evansville, Hanover, Taylor and Marian, and big schools like Indiana State, Notre Dame, Ball State, Butler and Purdue.

Indiana is a state with a rich Hoosier history. We have a Hoosier state flag, a state seal, a state song and a state bird. We even have a Hoosier state tree.

Cardinal

Tulip Tree

Peony

Before Indiana
became a state,
Native American
Indians
lived here.

Later,
settlers came
to our
land, and
they were
known as
pioneers.

OLD CORYDON STATEHOUSE, 1816-1825

In 1816, Indiana became our nation's 19th state.

Our state capitol started out in Corydon and moved to Indianapolis at a later date.

INDIANA STATEHOUSE, INDIANAPOLIS, INDIANA

Benjamin Harrison

William Henry Harrison

Abe Lincoln once lived in Indiana, and two other Presidents lived here, too.

Other famous Hoosiers include astronauts, actors, athletes, writers, inventors, singers and five Vice Presidents, just to name a few.

VIRGIL "GUS" GRISSOM

DAVID LETTERMAN

OSCAR ROBERTSON

JOHNNY APPLESEED

COLE PORTER

JANE PAULEY

WILBUR & ORVILLE WRIGHT

MADAM C.J. WALKER

JAMES DEAN

DON MATTINGLY

SCATMAN CROTHERS

DAN QUAYLE

JULIA CARSON

JAMES WHITCOMB RILEY

ORVILLE REDENBACHER

The word Hoosier is a mystery.
No one knows where it comes
from for sure.

But whatever a Hoosier used to be,
we all know what a Hoosier is today.

A Hoosier is someone with Indiana roots,
someone who loves our state in every way.

Hoosiers come in all shapes and sizes – all races and all creeds.

Some Hoosiers don't even live in our state. Over time, some Hoosiers do leave.

Because the key to being a Hoosier...
is having a big Hoosier Heart.

What is a Hoosier?

For well over a century and a half the people of Indiana have been called Hoosiers. It is one of the oldest of state nicknames and has had a wider acceptance than most. True, there are Buckeyes of Ohio, the Suckers of Illinois and the Tarheels of North Carolina — but none of these has had the popular usage accorded Hoosier.

But where did Hoosier come from? What is its origin? We know that it came into general usage in the 1830s. John Finley of Richmond wrote a poem, "The Hoosier's Nest," which was used as the "Carrier's Address" of the *Indianapolis Journal*, Jan. 1, 1833. It was widely copied throughout the country and even abroad. Finley originally wrote Hoosier as "Hoosher." Apparently the poet felt that it was sufficiently familiar to be understandable to his readers. A few days later, on Jan. 8, 1833, at the Jackson Day dinner in Indianapolis, John W. Davis offered "The Hoosher State of Indiana" as a toast. And in August, former Indiana Gov. James B. Ray announced that he intended to publish a newspaper, *The Hoosier*, at Greencastle, Indiana.

A few instances of the earlier written use of Hoosier have been found. The word appears in the "Carrier's Address" of the *Indiana Democrat* on Jan. 3, 1832. G. L. Murdock wrote on Feb. 11, 1831, in a letter to Gen. John Tipton, "Our Boat will [be] named the Indiana Hoosier." In a publication printed in 1860, *Recollections…of the Wabash Valley*, Sanford Cox quotes a diary which he dates July 14, 1827, "There is a Yankee trick for you — done up by a Hoosier." One can only wonder how long before this Hoosier was used orally.

As soon as the nickname came into general use, speculation began as to its origin. Among the more popular theories:

• When a visitor hailed a pioneer cabin in Indiana or knocked upon its door, the settler would respond, "Who's yere?" And from this frequent response Indiana became the "Who's yere" or Hoosier state. No one ever explained why this was more typical of Indiana than of Illinois or Ohio.

• Indiana rivermen were so spectacularly successful in trouncing or "hushing" their adversaries in the brawling that was then common that they became known as "hushers," and eventually Hoosiers.

•There was once a contractor named Hoosier employed on the Louisville and Portland Canal who preferred to hire laborers from Indiana. They were called "Hoosier's men" and eventually all Indianans were called Hoosiers.

• A theory attributed to Gov. Joseph Wright derived Hoosier from an Indian word for corn, "hoosa." Indiana flatboatmen taking corn or maize to New Orleans came to be known as "hoosa men" or Hoosiers. Unfortunately for this theory, a search of Indian vocabularies by a careful student of linguistics failed to reveal any such word for corn.

• Quite as possible is a facetious explanation offered by "The Hoosier Poet," James Whitcomb Riley. He claimed that Hoosier originated in the pugnacious habits of our early settlers. They were enthusiastic and vicious fighters who gouged, scratched and bit off noses and ears. This was so common an occurrence that a settler coming into a tavern the morning after a fight and seeing an ear on the floor would touch it with his toe and casually ask, "Whose ear?"

Many have inquired into the origin of Hoosier. But by all odds the most serious student of the matter was Jacob Piatt Dunn, Jr., Indiana historian and longtime secretary of the Indiana Historical Society. Dunn noted that "hoosier" was frequently used in many parts of the South in the 19th century for woodsmen or rough hill people. He traced the word back to "hoozer," in the Cumberland dialect of England. This derives from the Anglo-Saxon word "hoo" meaning high or hill. In the Cumberland dialect, the word "hoozer" meant anything unusually large, presumably like a hill. It is not hard to see how this word was attached to a hill dweller or highlander. Immigrants from Cumberland, England, settled in the southern mountains (Cumberland Mountains, Cumberland River, Cumberland Gap, etc.). Their descendents brought the name with them when they settled in the hills of southern Indiana.

As Indiana writer Meredith Nicholson observed: "The origin of the term 'Hoosier' is not known with certainty. But certain it is that . . . Hoosiers bear their nickname proudly."

About the Author and Illustrator

Married in 2002, Luke and Jennifer Messer live in Shelbyville, Indiana, with their beloved young daughters and two West Highland White Terriers.

Luke Messer, a sixth-generation Hoosier, was born in Evansville and raised in Greensburg, Indiana. Luke graduated with high honors from Wabash College and Vanderbilt University School of Law. Luke is a partner in the Indianapolis law firm of Ice Miller, serving as a member of its Public Affairs Group.

At the end of 2006, Luke will complete his second term as State Representative for District 57, where he represented Shelby and Bartholomew counties. Luke's legislative work on high school drop out prevention (HEA 1347) has received national recognition and was featured in the *Time* magazine cover story "Drop Out Nation" and on the Oprah Winfrey Show.

Luke serves on the community resource committee of Gleaners Food Bank and is a founding board member of ChildShare Indiana, a faith-based, non-profit organization dedicated to finding homes for foster children through local congregations.

Born in Asheville, North Carolina, and raised in Northeast Tennessee, Jennifer Messer became a Hoosier in 2001 when she moved to Indianapolis, Indiana, and joined the law firm Barnes & Thornburg. Jennifer obtained a Bachelor of Science degree in political science and speech communication from the University of Tennessee, Knoxville and a law degree from the University of Tennessee College of Law.

In 2006, Jennifer started Eva Publishing LLC, which publishes entertaining, educational books for little learners and the adults who read to them. Jennifer is a member of the board of directors of Girls Inc. of Shelby County and is a founding board member of ChildShare Indiana.